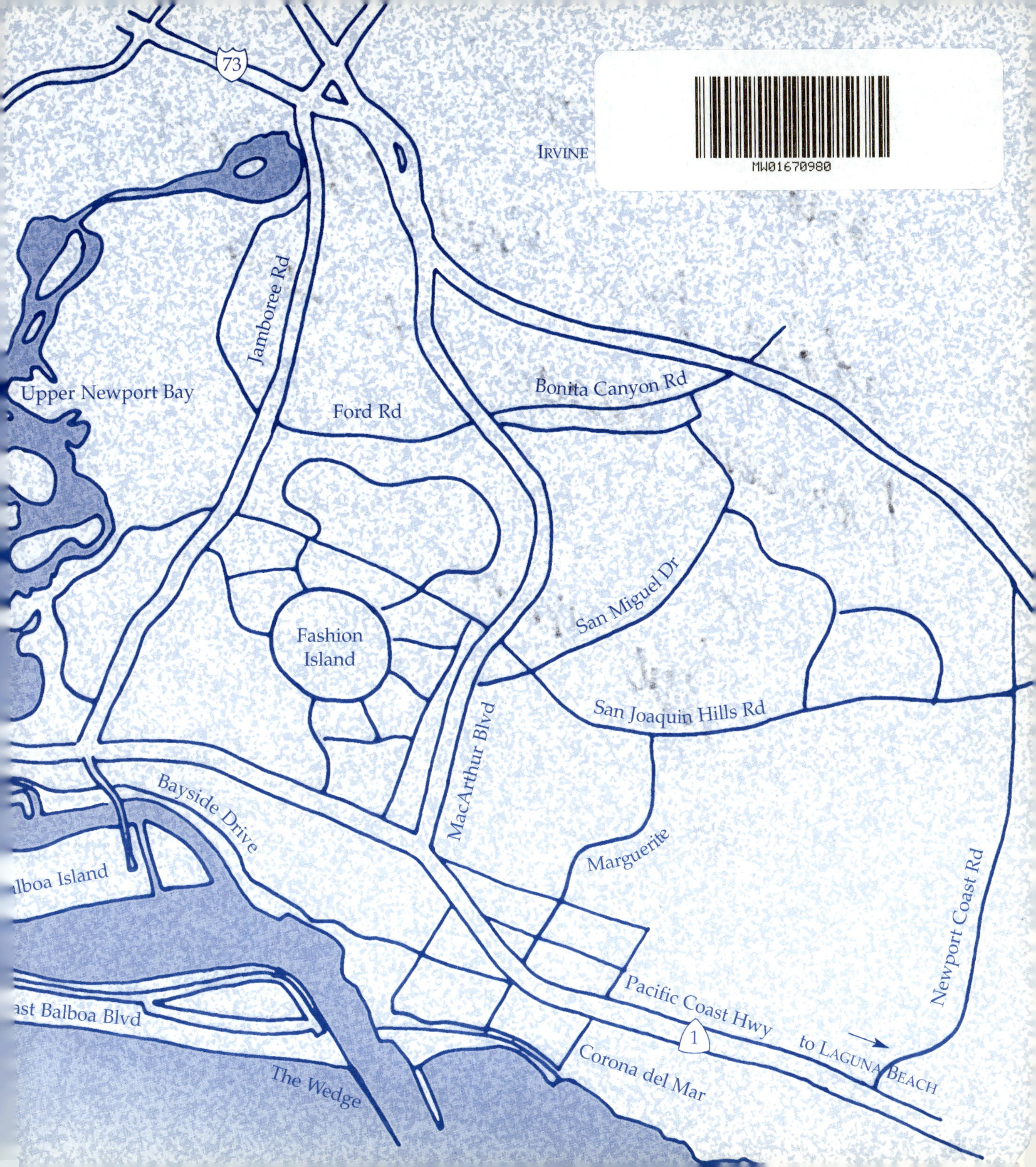
73
Irvine
Jamboree Rd
Upper Newport Bay
Ford Rd
Bonita Canyon Rd
San Miguel Dr
Fashion Island
San Joaquin Hills Rd
MacArthur Blvd
Bayside Drive
Marguerite
Newport Coast Rd
alboa Island
Pacific Coast Hwy
1
to Laguna Beach
ast Balboa Blvd
The Wedge
Corona del Mar

Congratulations!
Golden Bell - Best of the Best
Newport Beach, CA 2009

the Spirit of Newport Beach

original art and verse by Steve Simon

SIMON FINE ART

Published by:

Simon Fine Art
P.O. Box 34
Balboa Island, CA 92662

tel: 949-723-1100
www.stevesimon.com

ISBN 0-9652771-4-3

Edited by: Cheryl Russell

Manufactured in Singapore by Imago

To Leslie with love.
Here's to a special place we share in our hearts.

The Spirit of Newport Beach

City on the coast
Blessed with beach and bay
Resplendent beauty and the warm, sunny day,
And dawn's salty fog, effervescent of the sea
And ocean sunsets to calm you and me.

Where
Surfers dance 'top undulating waves
Lush green links pass golfers' days,
Pleasure yachts navigate a bustling bay
Tranquil wetlands put nature on display.
A stranger's greeting wears a smiling face
Wafts of jasmine relax the boardwalk's pace,
Rustling palms suggest a slight breeze
Pelicans patrol their lifeblood seas.

A place like none other I've found.
Indeed, a certain spirit does here abound.

North Bayfront (Balboa Island)
oil on canvas, 20 x 16 inches

Dockside Sailor

A morning stroll along a mellow bay

The ideal start to a wanderer's day.

Something here stirs the imagination

Of embarking on a bold exploration.

Idle sailboats await their next chance

To head out to sea, a timeless romance

Of man and sea, adventure and thrill

Nature's elements 'gainst savvy and skill.

Birds of a Feather

Plumage groomed, the day begun

Poised to salute the rising sun.

With a wiggle and a waddle along the plank

The platoon spaces out according to rank.

Two shakes of the leader's tail feather

And in they go, all at once and together.

Mallards in the Morning (Balboa Island)
oil on canvas, 14 x 11 inches

Balboa Pier
oil on canvas, 14 x 11 inches

The Tug of Time

Hulking and steadfast, a man-made pier
Anchored strong, nothing to fear.

But slowly the sea will claim as its own
This stilted beast with wood for bone.

Barnacles and mussels cling to her feet
Fog surrounds and waves ceaselessly beat.

And long after she stands no more
A beautiful wave will still break ashore.

Collision Course

One starts on a wave, the other on shore

Each the other pretending to ignore.

A certain collision course they share

Boyish bravado meeting girlish flair.

So begins the games they will play

A sport without end, played every day.

Boys Meet Girls (Corona del Mar)
oil on canvas, 11 x 14 inches

Koi Pond (Fashion Island)
oil on canvas, 14 x 11 inches

Something Fishy

Do they see what adults can no longer find?

Sure, I see the fish, but otherwise I'm blind.

Something about their excitement for everything

Makes me wonder what maturity did bring.

The fascination of all children, what could it be

For such intriguing things, adults simply cannot see?

Living a Fairy Tale

The ambience you won't soon be forgetting

A fairy tale writer would marvel at this setting.

It all seems designed by the Brothers Grimm

Gingerbread-like homes worthy of sugar-coated trim.

The camera won't do justice to the aura you feel

Photos have never proven a fantasy land real.

Crown Jewel (Corona del Mar)
oil on canvas, 24 x 18 inches

Crystal Cove Sunrise
oil on canvas, 12 x 9 inches

Open Invitation

It keeps me coming back time and again
Like an open invite from a good ol' friend.

This place I come to be alone
My mind adrift in a timeless zone.

But here I'm really not so far afield
For with each visit, something more's revealed
About myself I didn't realize before
Or conveniently chose to simply ignore.

And as I reflect upon the sunrise,
Be clearer still my foggy eyes.

Eureka!

Sure shopping is easier but isn't this more fun
To find something interesting the sea has spun.

Starfish, shells, and all sorts of finds
Unusual discoveries of all kinds.

Hey sis! Did you hear that sound?
You'll never believe what I just found!

Beachcombers (Balboa Island)
oil on canvas, 14 x 11 inches

Palms Bursting in Air (Corona del Mar)
oil on canvas, 15 x 30 inches

Anthem of a Pleasant Tandem

By the dawn's early light
Gentle aura and peaceful sight.

And the ocean's bright glare
With palms bursting in air,
Compel us in their own way
To feel joyful, come what may.

The mysterious power of sea and palm
To ease anxiety like a soothing balm.

It's All in the Name

Along a quaint street I slowly trod
Named for the flower of the goldenrod.

A palm attempted futilely with all its might
To shade my eyes from beaming sunlight.

A glorious goldenrod just the same
This unwitting mascot of the street's name.

Goldenrod (Corona del Mar)
oil on canvas, 12 x 9 inches

The King & His Court
oil on canvas, 14 x 11 inches

The Gatekeeper

The work will wait for another day
Grinning whilst you sail out the idle bay.

But before you begin your hooky afternoon
You check in with your buddies at "Sea Lion Saloon."

As usual, they're lettin' it all hang out
Drunk on seafood and sunshine, no doubt.

The glutton of the group strikes a macho pose
Chest protruded with upward pointing nose.

He approves your passing with his kingly opinion
You're now entering his noble dominion.

Lavender and Gold

There is a magical place, so I am told

Where life beams of lavender and gold.

I see a wildlife haven in my mind

Of flora and fauna of every kind.

Harmonious balance I feel in my soul

Yes, I believe in lavender and gold!

Back Bay Sunset
oil on canvas, 11 x 14 inches

On the Fence
oil on canvas, 14 x 11 inches

No Agenda

Passing the days, not a worry on his mind
Eating only the best, he's the finnicky kind.

He keeps no bedtime, nor time to rise
Just frequent cat naps to rest his eyes.

No need to work or even fetch the paper
He's quite simply a full-time mischief maker.

With a yawn and a stretch, outside he goes
What he's up to nobody knows.

Sun Worshippers

Beyond blooming aloe plants

Fronds of palms gently prance.

Strong and steadfast, passing each day

Indulgently soaking in each sun-filled ray.

Each drop of sun invigorating to the core

Full of warmth and energy galore.

Three Palms (Corona del Mar)
oil on canvas, 12 x 9 inches

Passing Time (Balboa Island)
oil on canvas, 24 x 30 inches

Quality Time

Let's load up the car with all the gear
Grab some snacks and head for the pier.

For surely there could be no lesser crime
Than missing out on such quality time.

And if we catch nothing the whole, live-long day
We'll just tell tales of the one that got away.

It's a Big World Out There

Down the path and to the sea

Unbridled childhood glee.

With a peek and a poke

They laugh and they joke.

But who will be the one to discover

Something more interesting than the other.

Sibling tidepoolers marveling at creation

Ah, the simple joy of exploration.

Tidepoolers (Corona del Mar)
oil on canvas, 14 x 11 inches

Three Alternatives
oil on canvas, 11 x 14 inches

Decisions, Decisions

Such an unfair quandary as this

To choose one and the other two miss.

I suppose either way you really can't lose

No matter the direction you finally choose.

A crossroads made to select your bliss

Only if all decisions were just like this!

Venerable Charm

Engineered as practical transportation

She's at least an equal part recreation.

What is it about her simple locomotion

Which so universally stirs emotion?

Like a steam locomotive's romantic appeal

I marvel at her rugged grace and nostalgic feel.

Whistle blows, she rumbles to the far shore

Where I look forward to ride once more.

Balboa Island Ferry
oil on canvas, 30 x 40 inches

Early Birds (Balboa Peninsula)
oil on canvas, 12 x 24 inches

Wake Up Call

On the beach, morning bright
Soft haze and golden light.

Waves on ocean casually riding
Cool shadows and shorebirds gliding.

Of soothing rhythm, harmonious scene
Vivifying aroma and beauty serene.

Something Brewing

Aromatic wafts of roasted coffee bean

Permeate the ambience of the scene.

A passerby bites at the sultry temptation

Of a cup of "joe" and friendly conversation.

In he goes, unassuming and discreet

What will he find, whom will he meet?

Coffee House (Cannery Village)
oil on canvas, 14 x 11 inches

The Wedge
oil on canvas, 11 x 14 inches

Joy Ride

With a knack for sensing a wave's potential
He chooses by means quite unconventional.

When the sun glistens off a swell just right
He deems it blessed with the Almighty's light.

Here comes one now, and off he goes
Fearless and joyous in the secret he knows.

Some scoff at his faith in such divine confiding
But who knows? Perhaps God, too, likes surfriding.

The Ferris Wheel

An American icon built for thrill and fun

Best enjoyed under a warm, summer sun.

Indeed, what childhood would be complete

Without having taken a ferris wheel seat.

And, if you're an adult, feeling the stress

Perhaps this is your ticket to decompress.

Balboa Fun Zone
oil on canvas, 14 x 11 inches

Island Entrance
oil on canvas, 14 x 11 inches

Island Welcome

Flags wave a welcome of wistful grace

Palms stand guard to a magical place.

Over the bridge and onto the isle

You can't help but crack an easy smile.

For not many a locale creates the sensation

Of feeling as if you're on permanent vacation.

It's in His Eyes

Some say our souls are born with a quest

To pursue, in life, what we do best.

And if the eyes are the window to the soul

Here we shall discover one's sincerest goal.

The look in his eyes needs no explaining

For he's clearly a cowboy in training.

Cowboy in Training (Balboa Fun Zone)
oil on canvas, 14 x 11 inches

Golden Years (Balboa Peninsula)
oil on canvas, 14 x 11 inches

The Gilded Path

A cup of coffee and the day's begun

Then off for a walk into the rising sun.

Not as romantic it might seem to most

As cocktails at sunset along the coast.

But they prefer new starts of things

Dawn's light and the energy she brings.

La Vie en Rose

A delicate waft of fragrant rose
Fills the air, luring my nose.

As I approach, it does seem
Like I'm the prince in my dream.

Beyond the castle's wall, is my boat
At the ready, in the protective moat.

If only I could truly harness the power
Of this magical dream weaving flower!

South Bayfront (Balboa Island)
oil on canvas, 14 x 11 inches

Big Corona
oil on canvas, 15 x 30 inches

Can't Wait til Summer

Today the beach is all their own

No one else in sight, all alone.

But it's only spring, a nip in the air

Still a few months of school to bear.

So they've begun with anticipation

The annual wait for summer vacation.

Upon Freedom's Perch

If I were a bird, if only I were

This is certain, this is for sure.

Freely I'd fly over my favorite coast

Landing only upon the rocks I liked most.

Where I'd greet friends old and new

Inquiring from where they just flew.

We'd share tall tales of our freedom trips

Favorite feeding spots and navigational tips.

And at the end of each of my shorebird days

Upon a sunset I would contently gaze.

Rocky Refuge
oil on canvas, 11 x 14 inches

Newport Pier
oil on canvas, 11 x 14 inches

Silver Lining

Beneath a somber, overcast sky

A surfer gallantly gives his best try

Before heading in as gulls stand by

While others take off and skittishly fly.

Though the sun peeks through, it simply won't stay

Nothing I can do nor words I might pray

To warm the spirit of this cool and dreary day

Besides seeing the beauty in all these shades of gray.

Siren's Song

Wind generously filling her elegant sails

Steersman monitoring her keen telltales,

Minding the tiller with a pro's knowing feel

Leaning to balance her gentle heel.

She's a siren of a beauty with the bold red hull

She's the tempting joy ride that never grows dull.

Santana 20
oil on canvas, 18 x 14 inches

Peninsula Park
oil on canvas, 14 x 11 inches

I'll Meet You There

A gazebo situated in an ideal location

Perfectly positioned for a main street celebration.

Imbued with a sense of the good ol' days

Childlike simplicity and innocent ways.

True to the essence of each plaza, park, or square

For people to unwind in a place they can share.

Hopeless Romantic

A colorful surprise for his beloved wife

Apple of his eye, partner for life.

Maybe she'd also like a fresh fruit treat

An orange, a nectarine, something sweet?

And who better the right choice to recommend

Than his loyal pal and otherwise best friend.

Farmers' Market (Corona del Mar)
oil on canvas, 11 x 14 inches

Walkin' the Dog (Balboa Peninsula)
oil on canvas, 14 x 11 inches

Cruisin' the Boardwalk

Sure, it connects this place with that location

But it really is its own destination.

Imagine a path made simply to enjoy the ride

Soaking in the sun, beach at your side.

So I'm reminded of advice I should apply

Enjoy the journey lest life pass you by.

The American Dream

Above each pier proudly on high

Stars and Stripes gallantly fly.

In each home a family with a story

Of unique meaning carried by Old Glory.

Each a small piece of a giant amalgamation

Of diverse peoples to form this great nation.

In the Spirit (Lido Island)
oil on canvas, 14 x 11 inches

Lookout Point (Corona del Mar)
oil on canvas, 24 x 18 inches

Remembrance

As a sailboat peacefully heads off to sea
I recall how much he meant to me.

Through my mind, childhood memories drift
One I cherish most, like the perfect gift,
Together we'd lower the flag at day's end
How lucky to have Dad as my best friend.

On the wings of a gull, a peace consumes me
Caressing my soul, all worry set free.
So I realize he's here at my side
Sharing moments, still on the ride.

And when we reunite, this suggestion I'll make
"Let's raise the flag for old time's sake!"

That Certain Something

Daylight the setting sun cannot elude

So this visit shall fittingly conclude

To a city blessed—one can see at first glance

With abundance, beauty, and riviera romance.

Ah, but amid these blessings there's something more

Not easy to explain but simple to adore.

A place like none other I've found

Indeed, a certain spirit does here abound.

Shorebirds (Corona del Mar)
oil on canvas, 9 x 12 inches

Simon Fine Art Gallery & Studio

Steve Simon's work may be seen at the artist's gallery and working studio on Balboa Island in Newport Beach, California.

Contact Information

Simon Fine Art Gallery & Studio
216 Marine Avenue
Balboa Island, CA 92662

toll-free ordering:
(877) 4CA-SCENES
(877) 422-7236

telephone: (949) 723-1100
facsimile: (949) 723-1650
e-mail: steve@stevesimon.com
website: www.stevesimon.com

Ordering Steve Simon *Original Art and Prints*

For availability of original art and prints of images reproduced in this book, please contact the Simon Fine Art Gallery & Studio. Contact information is on the preceding page.

A comprehensive presentation of items available from this collection, as well as other Steve Simon originals, reproductions and books, may also be viewed by visiting: http://www.stevesimon.com.

Other titles by Steve Simon include:
California: Through an Artist's Eye
Orange County: Through an Artist's Eye
Newport Beach: Celebrating 90 Years

List of Plates

Newport Beach, California

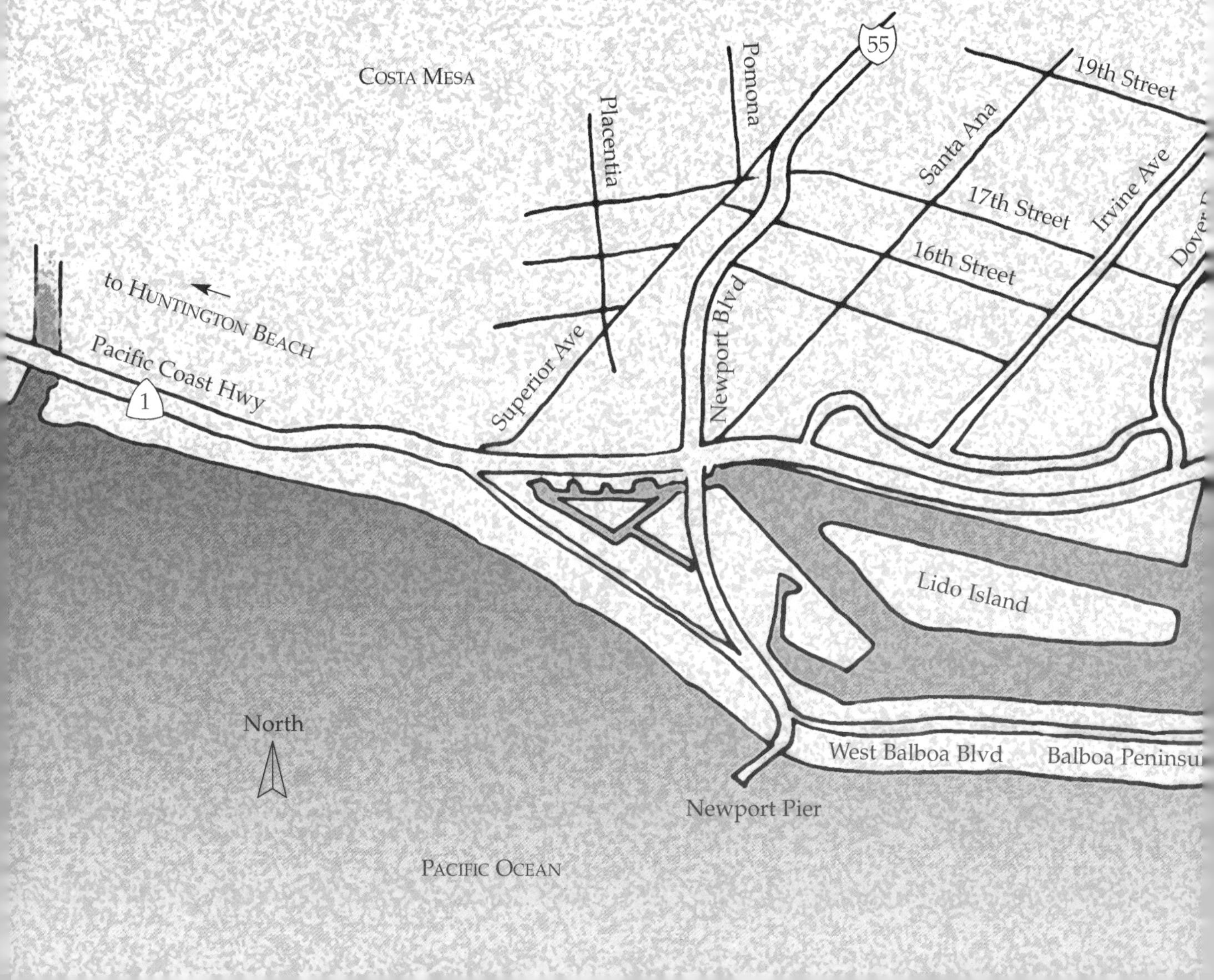